Vivisect

Lisa Lewis

New Issues Poetry & Prose

A Green Rose Book

New Issues Poetry & Prose
The College of Arts and Sciences
Western Michigan University
Kalamazoo, Michigan 49008

First Edition, 2010.

ISBN-10:   1-930974-92-2 (paperbound)
ISBN-13:   978-1-930974-92-0 (paperbound)

Library of Congress Cataloging-in-Publication Data:
Lewis, Lisa
Vivisect/Lisa Lewis
Library of Congress Control Number: 2010924162

Art Direction: Barbara Loveland
Design: Michele Hofe
Production: Paul Sizer
                   The Design Center, Frostic School of Art
                   College of Fine Arts
                   Western Michigan University
Printing: McNaughton & Gunn, Inc.

Vivisect

Lisa Lewis

New Issues

WESTERN MICHIGAN UNIVERSITY

Vivisect

Also by Lisa Lewis

Contents

I.

Morning Snowfall

Something tumbles through the snowy branches.
Branches near the tops of the pines are sagging:
The bottom limbs have melted clear, and the sky
Shimmers bright tundra. I didn't want to get up today.
Usually my sense of smell's no good so early,
But I pressed my face into the pillow, and there,
Perfume and cigarette smoke, my own.
I'd like to make a joke about that, but if I tried
To be funny I couldn't be drowsy, though
Sometimes I wake myself laughing. Strange—
I catch the end of it, like walking in on private
Conversation, and it stops, none of my business.
Last night snow thickened each twig
Of the bare maples. The winter grove
Glistened like a city. I knew today I'd see people
Taking mincing steps: old women can't walk
At all without giving little cries. My grandmother
Called like that when I was a small girl.
I understood nothing about her shrieks
Except they were like the sounds of a bird
You want to see anyway, though its voice
Is a disappointment. My mother was angry.
Once she and I were alone she'd say,
"Don't ever let me do that." I promised.
But when she started, I couldn't stop her.

What happens. What happens is all good. What
Happens is all bad. I look at it either way.
The creek in the pit of the ravine is too thick
To move; it's like the ice in machines
At convenience stores, churning weakly
Around and around a paddle. You can buy
Some and stick a straw in it. It's colored pink,
Or purple, to make you feel like a child.
You drag up the straw from the cup's bottom,
It's shaped like a spoon on the end, but ice is real,
There it is down the hill, no one invented that,
They noticed and wanted to taste without the mud.
If every snowflake is a dead soul, how many

Of us are there? I'm counting myself, I can't
Rest, I'll walk forever, alive or not. Later
This morning the mothers will bundle
Their toddlers in fat nylon jackets and scoot
Them out to play. They want them strong,
Hardened to the weather. They've got a lot of
Changing to do. I'm glad I got through it and
Can stay the same. Except it's harder than that.
After a while you have to do things to yourself
So people overlook the changes you can't
Stop. Like if snow covers the sidewalk—
You scrape it aside with a shovel, and the wet
Pavement shines brown, almost as if it were
A rainy day, which is more like being young.

It seems that some people don't know when
To die. I believe they must be looking out
At the weather and thinking, I'll never go
Under the snow, I'll wait till spring. Then
When spring comes, they think, I'll never
Give up the blossoming trees, I'll wait till
The terrible heat comes and makes me tired.
When I sit with my mother, she keeps waving
Toward the window. Someone asked her,
Do you know where you live? They wanted
A specific answer, a proper name. She said,
I live right here. They said, Do you know
Where your daughter is? She waved toward
The window and said, Out there. I don't find
Anything wrong with that. I know she thinks
I'm closer to death than she is. She always
Believed that and so did I. I'm too serious,
I must have thick ice clogging me up inside.
When I breathe bare branches rub
Crosswise in the wind. Or the cricket sings,
Which if you find in the house you know
Someone's dying that moment. My mother
Will never die, no matter what holes bore
Their way to her brain. She does everything right,
And what makes her mad is when people

Stand in her way. It happened at the hospital:
She couldn't understand why they wanted her
To lie in bed all day. It bothered her sleep, she
Demanded to know why. I put my arms
Around her; she whimpered a little; then
When I pulled away she glared. She
Doesn't like to be treated like that. She knows
If we're not arguing something's wrong.

Wind drifts the snow many directions. Wind
Tilts the slim trunks of poplars and elms.
Wind shaves the white fur of snow from bare
Boles: is that the kind of split we humans have
In our bodies, just something to live with?
We're born with ours. I don't think trees are born
Complete. They don't change fast, though every year
There are new branches. We start whole
As plastic dolls. We're pumped full of blood
And we keep swelling; we don't want to
Get bigger so we stop. I knew today I'd see
The man I'm watching on the other side
Of the ravine. He parked his red car too far
From the house. He has to get to it without
Hurting himself. He moves slowly,
Pretending it's wisdom making him take
Small steps, so he can look around calmly,
Judge the day, compare it to the other storms
He's observed in his long life. The snow falls
And everything changes. We have to be careful
Of holes in the earth, crevices brushed with snow:
They might be deep enough to break a leg.
They might draw us in right up to the heart.
Snow evens shallow graves. White hair
Sprouts over holes in the brain. We see what
We want, and everything changes along
With the day, sunspot faded to whiteness
Now, white sky, white branches, white hair
Tangled on the white pillow that smells

Of white, clean the way she likes it, white
Like the snow she can't see and white
Like the holes we can't see. We only know
The danger of falling if we move fast.
So we move so the snow almost fills
Our footsteps before we look back.
That's dangerous too, a design to get lost
When the world's all white and nothing
Looks like it did last summer, when you
Could tell what tree you were standing under
By the honey and color of its blossoms.

Only A Little

I hear lots of stories about people who have it rough.
I claim it's compassion making me listen close,
But I'm playing a game of comparison: suffering's
Secret wages amount to nothing hoarded, but there's
A penalty for saving when they're spent. To say
You've suffered, you have to look the part. But you
Can't come out with everything on top of years
Of passing for untroubled. Maybe I don't give
Anyone more than partial credit. There's a reason
I'm not the kind of person conversations
Are reported to: "John said you're the saddest person
He ever got so sick of," or such like. Maybe everyone's
Got it sewed up, my sack of innuendo: I wasn't
Quick to figure out I was an unwed mother's child,
Though nothing added up to say I wasn't. Since
I'm no longer a child at all, it seems too late to talk
About it. But sometimes it's like what my grandfather
Wanted the day he had the bandages off and new glasses
After cataracts: he asked to be driven around town
To the scenes he thought he'd seen. He grabbed
My mother's arm at a crosswalk. "Baby," he said,
"The light is green." It wasn't he was in a hurry.
He hadn't noticed the light before. So after I worked up
My nerve to ask her—I had to try it over the phone,
Seven states between us—and realized she'd waited
To be asked the question she'd chosen,
Maybe decades before, I set the receiver back
In the cradle and walked outside to look around.
At the roses weighing down tips of brittle canes.
Mud where I stepped out cigarettes. Clouds
Unbuckling their belts in the heat. Poorly
Dressed children walking home from school,
Swinging plastic bookbags. The hoods of cars
In sunburned brights barreling down from the stoplight.
It was going to cost to tell what I could see.
It was a little different. But only a little.

The End Of Anything

Night after night I woke to the stuck whoop
Of a car alarm, far enough away I couldn't spot it
To call the cops. Between Marty's snores
It sounded overheard. The last years of our marriage,
We moved to a family neighborhood, farther
From the Galleria where young men hoping
To come off wealthy parked leased Audis
And hitched rides with suited glass ceiling
Women they singled out in bars. Prowlers,
Perhaps feral cats, brushed high tails
On burnished bumpers and set off the basic
Shriek of alarms or, uncommonly, a recorded
Voice STAND AWAY FROM THE CAR:
The decade of Robocop, presumed safe
From the future it kept guessing right.
Lying under the leaky roof of a rent house,
Street of flood and fire ants, I thought of
My books stacked by legal pads, notes
On the prosody of *Samson Agonistes*
For a late term paper, and the cycle
Of sound whirred on without me, sirens,
Motors, shouted words in Spanish, translated
START, STOP, START. It might've been a whole
World out there, a globe of one smooth continent,
Workers polishing mirrored surfaces, whirling
Paddles, air forced through reeded apertures.
I opened my arms to Marty's thatched back
And felt it frozen in fur. I dreamed of my next
Dark motive, to have a child, get noticed
Swelling in the belly and breasts,
But that wouldn't be the end of anything,
And candlelight described a flickering shadow
I could not stare straight. In public I foreswore,
Foreclosed. Anyone who gazed into my eyes
Said it was over for me, I made it so
Slamming knives into secret tables,
Sticking them up on their points as in movies.
In real life I've never seen it work.

Maybe I'd even have to get up and stretch
My long sore arms over my head before

The circular intrusion of car alarm whipped
Open, lost its note, collapsed like dropped
String. I'd bought a weight set to improve
My independence, but it tired me lifting
Myself alone, imagining the western haze
Of the future, my life as petrified ostrich egg.
Fingertips, clitoris, bulb of the nose, extended
Tongue; balloon stomach, gall bladder's summer
Gourd, kneecap's castile. I've left out the circular
Logic of my divorce, when I edited my bad words
And his bad words and the bad words on TV.
Ten years we crouched like pandas raised
Captive so they don't know how to mate,
The decade newspapers described cocooning
And I bought lampshades designed by faceless
Workers I intended to dream anyway.
By the time I could believe it, another planet
Was born of dust, and there I was, meteorite,
A spume of sparks same as every other hope.
I don't remember the great-aunt's name
Who kept the garden and cold royal blue steel ball,
Or the blind collie's that licked my face
When I bent and laid both hands to its curves.
I only knew I was glad to get inside: adults
Nursed toddies and talked loud within the blue
Sphere I gave up calling the blue ball after boys
Claimed that term for what I never caused.
There was a kind of girl I swore I'd never be,
Teen princess waiting for Elvis at the train
Station, holding up posters, WE LOVE YOU ELVIS,
Like there wouldn't be thousands more
At the next whistlestop, like he'd be able to
Do anything even if he saw one he wanted,
Like he'd yell STOP THE TRAIN THAT GIRL
LOVES ME and the brakes would slam
The fleeting loaf of riveted metal to a halt
Before she disappeared into the night
Of her parents' home. I am not that kind of girl,

But when his fist closed around my neck
Like a stuffed animal and cast me back
On the bedspread I went limp and the dream
In my head was a globe, like the breasts
Of the exercise instructor in the video I bought,
Rising from her ribs like skinned coconuts.
I am not that kind of girl but should've been
If I wanted to be taken up inside a video
Or a roomy two-parent home.
I'm thin, fed on my own cruelty, never
Enough to go around, round out my dire
Little chest the young men ignored.
I'm razor, flour spilled on countertop,
Rib bone. But I'll take what I have coming.
I won't sit up night after night remembering
When I woke to car alarms and was as close
As I could get to what I couldn't get close to,
Not a husband but the idea of a husband,
A husband's reliable successors, a heavy head
Bowing over an open book, a garden implement,
Telephone, gravy boat, or any other object
A lucky man doesn't have to own to use.

For My Mother's Sleep

You told your stories too many times.
The girl in the dorm room playing
Frank Sinatra until you hid the record.
The mynah in the motel office you
Thought might've been the clerk
When it said "Hello." You took up
Your story-telling voice like a trance.
I don't think I'm going to hear it again.
I don't believe Grover really thought
It was funny, you whimpering like a child
In his arms after you had your stroke.
He can't help the way he talks to me,
Putting on that sardonic voice he tortured
Me with as a teenager. You remember.
Or maybe you don't. It's hard to think
Back to what you were doing, maybe
Stirring a pot on the stove, or shaking
Dirt from your gloves after gardening.
I can't talk about you in the hospital bed.
I don't know what I expected from
"Massive stroke." I don't like to use
Those words. That's not the right way
To talk about the body, as if it were a wall.

I'm going to make myself a little girl
Again. I'm going to remember how I felt
On the escalator at Miller and Rhodes
Department store, holding your hand
And hating it. I'm going to remember
Those expensive dolls, the ones in blue
Boxes you wouldn't let me touch. Then
We'd go to the lingerie department.
I'd run my hands over the bras on hangers,
Sidle up to the girdle display—I knew you
Wore one—and stretch the elastic
With both hands the way they did on TV.
The time you took me to the Tea Room
I was sick. I was skinny and pale,
And my long brown hair made me ugly.

You wore a brown suit with a velvet hat
And drew lipstick on in a mirror
So the waitress cleared the plates
Even though I hadn't had ice cream yet.
I was going to grow up like you. I was going to
Have a job like you. Someday I'm going to die
Like you. I wish you'd wake up for a while first,
But you can't. I don't believe Grover really
Thought it was funny, the way you slumped to
The living room floor. I know he wouldn't
Mean to laugh at you babbling like a baby.
I wish you'd come back to my apartment,
Take your furniture away. You brought designs
Into my house. You're going to give me a stroke.
You burst one of those snaky veins,
I have them too, all over. My arms look
Like a man's, vein and muscle. Yours
Are skinny and veiny, the veins crushed,
Needles sticking through. They've got
Dry rot, it's not good, they're going to
Burst all over you. Then what will we do?

That week I drove away from my husband,
You and I talked late, and it seemed too
Important, like a last time. You're old.
I knew what that meant. But you visited me
In this apartment. You propped
Your skinny legs on the coffee table.
I watched your fat belly in pink terrycloth,
You on the sofa filing your nails.
I watched your head nodding, hair thin on top,
Puffed up to hide it. I got angry with you
Like I always do, but you were too deaf
To argue. I talked a lot about my husband.
I'd believed leaving him would make me
A girl, and surprise, it started to work:
I was eager as when you'd pick me up
Friday afternoons, always impatient,
I'd hurry to the car, you had things to do.
It's not that I wish I'd told my secret,

How to follow my example. Nothing
Could bring you back whole now,
You'd gone too far already.
Nothing saved me in my body either.
All the veins stayed the same in my heart,
Some of them tighter, thinner. Nothing's
Bringing either one of us back. Nothing's
Really different. I don't wish you'd tell
Those stories about the girls you met at college
And how you were friends for life. I heard
Those stories a million times, and you didn't
Tell them well. I just can't remember them.
Ask me some questions. Raise your head.
Tell me again the first thing
I loved in the world.

Competition

It's August. A cicada in the chimney
Where swallows nest in spring.
Dust on the lampshade, crack turned
To the wall. A woman writing for
Company. One of her troubles is
Reluctance; the other is knowing.
I know her well, but I'm someone
Else. I know her troubles, but mine
Are different. She's wearing a scarf.
I don't even own a scarf. It's too hot
For a scarf, August in Oklahoma.
The woman in the scarf misunderstands
Heat and wants more when she has
Enough. Perhaps she intends to store it
For dark times. She prefers to be seen
In silhouette against white stucco
Palm-frond swept. She writes
Of a picnic in August. Tablecloth
From birthday party, purple elephants,
Chartreuse hot air balloons.
Canned baked beans in a metal bowl.
Croquet mallet, sliced strawberries.
She wears rings, and a scarf,
And when no one's looking
She takes off the rings and peers
Through them like lenses, like a scope.
She doesn't want to see anything
Outside a long stalk of light.
Between her two cool hands
It's not going to burn anybody.
My problem is entirely different.
I'm not even in the room with her.
I tried the door on an old building,
I'm not sure where, the knob
Came off when I tugged hard,
I stayed locked out. And it's August,
So hot and gold the dogs have
Lapped up all the answers.
You could look all over the ground
For a word to direct you and just
Live lost or get smarter. She wants

Nothing to do with me. She knows
I'll prowl this corner and keep her
In front of the mirror she painted
On the wall where she writes
To remind her how to look inside
Out. My problem is this fire
Smelling of gods that gives me
Away no matter how I hide.
My problem is the shrill note
Of my whistle when I call the owls
To frighten her awake,
To crawl in the open windows
And dismember mice
On the pages of her journals.
I know she's writing about me.
She's spent most of the evening
Thinking of how to describe me.
I can't let anyone know what
She thinks of me. She knows
The names of the cut flowers
And dissolves aspirin in water
Before she bathes their wounds.
My problem is I never spent
A night away from her before,
And I'm waiting to show her
My face in the morning, bloody
Slaps where mosquitoes lit,
The words on my lips knowing
Of her knowing, my guilty eyes
I'll try to make her look away
From, first, as dogs do, children,
And politicians; and, among grown
Women, both wives and whores.

Neurological Progressive Care

That family is here every time I'm here.
We recognize each other, but we don't speak.
The nurses keep us waiting past our appointed
Hour. Then they let us in, two at a time,
And we go to the sink to wash up. That family
Wanted to bring flowers, they're not allowed.
They left a vase at the nurses' station. That family
Stands at the foot of the loved one's bed, a middle-
Aged man still looking strong and handsome
Lying there with his eyes closed, the relatives
Telling jokes and glancing up at the TV.
My mother says there's a fish tank
Over the refrigerator door and nods
Her head that way. Her wisdom is beyond
Knowing. The oxygen cannula whispers
Oracular prophecy, *look out the window,*
The narrow window, see the pigeons rise
Together above the room where your mother's
Heart scrawls a crooked line, visitors are leaving
The building early, carrying daisy vases
The nurses forgot to water, look out the window.
My mother says, That man peed on the sheets.
She makes a face. The nurse vacuums her throat
With a clear tube. I wish she'd close her eyes
Like that man with the big family. I wish
She'd dream she was loved like him, he doesn't
Even speak and look how they come to him,
They bring him gifts that are turned away.
All she has is a daughter who has come a long way
On no money. I'm going to listen to every word
She says. Tonight she is stripped to her true
Genius. Look out the windows, lower the lights,
We're mourning in here, these strangers,
My mother, the man whose eyes rest whole
As almonds inside their brittle shells. This is
Our business, to guard the bodies, which guard
The mystery we want the key to. Look out
The window. Visitors are leaving the building
Early. That family is carrying something.
You can hear them all the way up here.
A woman says she thought she noticed
The slightest pressure from his hand.

The History Of Sexuality

She's not herself. When she crawled onto the roof to hang
The banners, tassels sticking to her sweaty legs,
She remembered a lamed goddess balancing scales.
It was a mistake to hide weapons in the cottonwood grove
And climb the hill to view the landscape's folds like giant's
Skin, part machine like in the movies, or the hospital, sliding
Down pain into vision, scientist's euphoria blurring clouds:

No answer. Known harmony rang the branches
Of the brooks and dark-boled elms, bergamot scent,
Inessential as folk tale: known memory of touch,
Resignation, flints dipped in poison staining the quiver.
The secret congregation gathered in the firelight of promise.
Each tremor foiling the night tracked prayer,
Sacrifice, sexual confusion—

No such thing. You want to argue. I can feel you days away,
Flowing on the river of rage where I can't watch, forcing
Along campers' trash, detritus of summer, silt, minnows.
You'd take my shoulders and shake them like enemies,
Here in the depths of distance I swore one morning in the sun
I'd use like a wire to set the susurrus running again. It glowed
In my hand, it glowed around my footsteps, I paced afire.

She's not herself. You're not yourself. Nowhere to find,
Either of you, longing useless against absence, the shudder up
Your spine when I summon you against your will and, run, you go
Again—both of you, girl hanging flags and heartless traveler,
You talking circles around her, last place you left her, returning,
Grown child to the family home. Love was a brother's enemy
In that life, you couldn't tell, but she guessed; she got it

Out of you so you fled. She's not herself. I've opened her thighs
While she slept. Everyone does; she never knows.
She never told me she was turning to water. She said
She was turning to agate, sine arcs of rust and jade. She never
Said she was turning to fire. She claimed no ink played
On the cave walls in winter when she couldn't catch cold without
Dying the last time. You're not yourself or you'd go where she is.

You're not yourself, who are you anyway, going away, taking
The fire and the money, going away? All I can tell you she said is
She'd walked to the place where everyone turns back,
And the water blossoms with gold fire, squinting
Like a day out of school, still just kids
No matter how you hurt them. They make sure to scream
In the woods so they won't get in trouble, and now look

What's happened: we don't scream, we don't get in trouble,
But our hearts are weaker than violets, and we're dreaming
Of carrying a roll of silk to the mountaintops we can't get to
Without letting go and drinking fire, to save money,
Or orphan children, whoever they are. We're dreaming
Of planting a flag. We climbed a peak, we snapped branches,
We dreamed the way to one another's dream. Oh, it was embarrassing,

Not to be able to tell my love from her love from your love
From the fear that woke us, curled in separate cupboards like bears,
Or witches, pallid from handing up magic. It only changed us a little.
Even we wish it had dropped us dead like the label says.
Our hands are full of needles and piano keys, and when we touch
Another body it dies from lack of sleep, lack of love. Do you know
What you did? You feel me finding out secrets,

The answer to what happened? She's not herself.
She knew we'd touched her when she climbed onto the roof.
She felt us forcing her body down. You took one shoulder,
I the other, we gave her our tongues, our teeth to tear
Our throats out. She knew we'd touched her when the cottonwood
Emptied its pouch down to the worm in the seam. You were gone.
You'd never be caught. I was the friend who believed.

Media

I keep trying to get my friend on the phone but the line's busy.
Pretty soon she'll be putting her little boy to bed; there's no use
Calling then. She lies next to him till he drifts off; usually
She does too. They tuck into his bunk bed like darner's pins
Gathering the eastern horizon, so far below where the sun
Comes up the wrinkle doesn't show in the southern plains.
That's where I'm pacing my living room, thinking about
What I'd like to tell my friend, mostly what another friend
Has said, and what I think will happen next in the drama
That shouldn't even interest me, it's just petty, local intrigue—
Really, what must my friend think? It probably looks like
I'm desperate—the word people use to ward off terror
Of making it to middle age without someone so long reliable
It's merely predictable when he comes on to the boss
Or the boss's secretary after just one drink at the Christmas
Party. "What is she, desperate?" I used to sneer, sizing up
A pairing that reminded me of my secret fear I'd have to
Marry someone who asked me, not someone I wanted.
That was a marriage and divorce ago. I'd say they were
Like waves breaking on a beach except I never glistened
White like a beach and no one searched me for treasure.
I knew nothing of despair when I saw it everywhere
And shrank until it passed me by. It takes being found out
As the one with the bruise or fontanel, the terrifying
Vulnerability the stab of a thumb could pulp, to use up
The time, or the shelter, or the light by which to see.
Tonight, though, getting directions isn't the problem.
Despair looms like a mountain closing in on a highway—
No, wait, it's the other way around, a fast-moving sedan
Heading for the tunnel entrance bored in the forested slope—
And I'm going to wait here forever as car after car
Crashes in what turns out to be an optical illusion, there's
No tunnel entrance and no tunnel and the highway sent us
All here by accident so no one can be held accountable
For those many deaths, their inevitability, or the loneliness
Of the dying, who know the day they're born their fate
Awaits them here in this carefully laid trap; they live
Toward impact, fierce to force away anyone who might
Come near to offer a little kindness, maybe a touch, before

Flame the size of a broken heart starts straight up through
The moving image, the film ends, and the crowd goes home.
My world of solace is as distant as ever, spinning away
With me on it, waving my spindly arms, a light year every
Beep of the busy signal, my friend's words, her very breath
Punctuating cycles of madness, misery, loneliness and despair,
So far away nobody could possibly know about it, let alone
Care, even when they're well within earshot, I'm talking
Directly to them, explaining as calmly as I know how.

Tracy and Joe

You don't want to know how quiet my life's become
That last night when I heard someone scream *Whore!*
It was one in the morning and I was so bored
With black-and-white sitcoms on the all-night station
I hit the mute button on the remote control,
Sidled to the window, and parted the curtains
Just a slice so no one would see me but I could watch
What was going on and do something about it
If it came to that—call the cops, step outside and hope
My mere presence would settle the fight, if that's what
It was; and it was, all right. Two young men
Pursued a woman, their silhouettes in streetlight,
Her permed hair. Her red sports car was parked
Against the curb. "I'm not lying, Joe!" Her voice
Was shaking. "Don't talk down to me!" Joe was
The tall one, in droopy jeans. "Fucking whore!"
Joe shouted, and the short guy, slight, started
Screaming too: "Pussy! Cunt!" Then my own voice:
"Stop fucking with her!" I didn't care if they heard.
I wanted to fight and get it over with. I saw
The woman run to the car. The men turned back
To the little blue house. I flipped the phone book
To the police station number. I closed it back
And poured a drink of water. One-fifteen. I thought
About sleeping. Then I heard they were at it again.
This time I opened my front door, slowly. I saw
The woman fling her car door wide, jump in
Like an arrow drawn to its target, click on the lights
And peel out into the street. Behind her the men
Stood waving their fists. "Whore! Cunt! Pussy!"
Then they lowered their voices. Tracy, they called her.
Called her "whore" again. "Did you fuck her?"
The tall one, Joe, challenged. "No, man, I wouldn't
Do that to you!" the slim one objected. "Have you
Got a cigarette?" Joe handed one over. "You
Wouldn't fuck her if she spread her legs? Could you
Stop? With her laying right there in front of you?"
The short guy tried to change the subject.
"Come on, let's be friends. What are you

Pissed off about? You got your way." He said it
Bitterly. "Stupid girls! They spread their legs
And you put your dick between them!" The night
Was quiet. Every word was clear. It was easy
To understand what he meant. Women spread
Their legs. Men put their dicks between them.
They think they can't stop. That's how it seems.
Maybe they want the stopping to start before
Anything else does. They don't say so. Maybe they
Think they're doing a favor. Maybe they think
There'll be gratitude later. Maybe they feel sorry
For someone lonely. Maybe they want the sense
Of adventure. Maybe they want to be told they're
Good. Maybe they think they love someone.
I watched the young men. They stopped talking.
I wondered where the woman had fled for comfort.
Today a man parked a car I'd never seen in the drive
Of Joe's little house. He stared out the window,
His forehead glowing. Was he one of them?
I couldn't tell. In the hot afternoon I watched
Through the blinds till my vision wavered. Then
The phone rang, a credit card company, and when
I came back the driveway was empty. I hadn't heard
The engine start or a car door slam. It was quiet
Everywhere, wind sweeping birdsong
Into the empty street. I'm not afraid. But I know
Truth when I hear it. Tracy peeling out
Into the night where now you'd never guess
That drama played here, and I memorized the lines
Like I'd already heard them a thousand times.

Christmas Eve

If, twenty years ago, someone had told me
That December 24, 1997, I'd spend the day
Alone, unhurried, in the morning buying
A book, *Raising Poultry the Modern Way*,
For my oldest friend, I seldom see her now
She's married and a mother in rural North
Carolina, and I'm married to my job, as people
Used to say, pityingly and warily, of women
Like me, sometimes men too, or married to my
Horse, as a woman I know from the stable
Jokes about herself, also married to her job;
And then in the soggy afternoon driving
To the stable and riding my horse, whose neck
And haunch are thickening now she's almost
Four, learning to jump, today we raised the bar
And didn't knock it down a single time, also

The half-pass, *begin in shoulder-fore, stay*
Rounded in sitting trot, don't let the haunches
Lead, stretch the outside leg as far back as you
Must to hold the wandering haunches on track,
Release the foot from the stirrup if need be
And nudge with the spur, Jeanie always gives
A little grunt, I always feel a little sorry,
I always wonder if I really needed to push her
So hard, if she might not listen to the heel
Alone, except I know better, I try sometimes
And all precision is lost; and later still,
In the chilly evening dismounting and wiping
Sweat from Jeanie's sides and feeding her
Lump sugar, wondering if she understands
I'm thanking her for her willing performance,
Today without distraction from other riders,
Who have all gone to their respective homes
To celebrate the holidays, leaving me to work
In the stable another hour or so, trundling
The red plastic cart from stall to stall, sliding
Beside it to enter next to the horses others own,
Speaking to each of them, their faces masked

In padded winter hoods but their ears active,
Their eyes alert, and shoveling out the day's
Manure, also my task tomorrow, so the stable
Owner moves uneasily around me, grateful,
It's obvious, someone's around who'll take
The job no one else will do, but also sorry
To have to ask me, embarrassed to leave
For his gifts and dinner, his fourth wife,
Children, and parents, who live next door
In the old farmhouse where he grew up,
Later he bought a mobile home and parked it
Yards away, so his son plays where he once
Played, his stepdaughters play where he once
Played, he tries to make their lives fuller
Than his, or as he imagines his was not full,
He was an only child, as I was, and he knows
What's wrong with growing up alone, perhaps
Not so convinced as I it turns out for the best—
I would've said, *Of course, how could it be*
Any other way, damn straight I'll be alone,
I'll be the weirdo, fucking aye, what else
Would you expect from someone fathered
By a rapist?—except I couldn't've said it,
I didn't know yet, not twenty years ago,
My mother having opted for the seemingly
Noble keeping of secrets, told me she'd been
Divorced, someday I'd understand, apparently
Forgetting I'd wonder why there'd been no
Mention of child support, let alone visits
Or alimony, but I took decades to work up
The nerve to ask outright what really
Happened; besides, it would've been a vicious
Thing to say, even if true, even if I knew,
Because in youth I hoped for normalcy,
Fitting in, and I cast around to fit with people,
Not the kids who tormented me demanding,
Who's your father? Where's he live? and not
The kids who broke into houses, shot up heroin,
And dragged me along to take the blame,
And not the girls who rode horses too but then

My mother married Grover and we had to move
Away, and not the ballet and merchandising
Majors at the women's charm-school college
I attended for a degree in horsemanship
And slept with two of my professors instead,
So if I'd had the remotest idea, all my efforts
Would be in vain, that despite the work
Of reconciling my strangeness with the habits
Of the rest of the world, practiced as it seemed
To be at staying the same, always the same,
I would've let my redneck boyfriend hurt me
More than I did, more than pulling out chunks
Of my hair and kicking me in the ribs, and I
Would've worried when I failed at the jobs
I took the year I finished college, would've
Thought it darkest prophecy I couldn't sell
Glassware door to door, couldn't lie or change
The subject when someone challenged my canned
Patter but followed my usual inclinations
And blushed and fell silent in exposed shame
To slink back to my car, brochures in hand,
And I might've injected my arm full of air,
Needle tilted over the pumped-up vein one night
In a bathroom where a diabetic had left her
Equipment after doing what she needed to keep
Herself alive, though I read in our alumni
Newsletter months ago she'd died, no cause
Named but I guessed her disease had been worse
Than she wanted her classmates to know,
Her signature perky cheerfulness concealing
Certainty I doubt I could've hidden, and I might've
Died from an air bubble, the one cc. I'd heard
From my friends who shot up dope was enough
For embolism, or worse, it might've had no effect,
I might've only humiliated myself, given myself
A major pain in the neck or wherever the cc.
Lodged before dissipating, as it surely must,
Even on a corpse, through the permeable

Walls of the vessel, and if I'd died, I wouldn't've
Discovered that the long struggle I lived
To be normal was a waste of my energies only
Insofar as it didn't work to make me fit in
But otherwise taught me something different
Than people know who grew up with parents,
Brothers, and sisters, a clear design to play out
The drama they've trusted all along. So today
What I knew is how comical, how fierce, how
Entirely *possible* it is to drive alone on Christmas
Eve without the faintest remonstrance in mind
Against commercialism ruining the spirit
Of the season or other rhetorical loyalty
To the Christian practice I never believed in
Because its emphasis on holy fathers excluded
The facts I knew of beginning or else included
Them in ways I couldn't mention, I must be
The Christ child myself, the savior, and maybe
I still get a kick out of knowing I once entertained
Such provocative notions in familial secrecy,
Sensing the dilemma, already wise as my mother
Had to be in the ways of protecting myself
From the outrage of those who can't be blamed
For defending ideas they'll live for good
Against the disproof of someone like me, now
Married to my job, married to my horse, laughing
Off starlight of Christmas Eve, inside where it's
Warm, the space heater's on, glancing out
The window, remembering the houses I passed
Hours ago, knowing the rituals soon to begin,
Remembering the unspoken dissatisfactions,
Not free of them but now at a distance, on this
Evening otherwise like any evening, my legs
Tired from riding, fingers calloused from the reins,
Tomorrow to do it all over again, the solitary
Waking, coffee and Kools, drive to the stable,
Saddle marks to groom, nothing special about
The shit I'll shovel, nothing new in the thoughts
I'll think, nothing terrible about the way
It turned out, except how I make other

People nervous, now mostly their problem,
Which they'll feel when they turn up tomorrow
Wearing caps and sweaters their relatives
Bought them, which I don't have, and those
Who haven't lived like this don't know it's not
So bad, but they believe it's rude to enjoy
Their fortune right in front of my deprived face,
So I'll stand back and watch them swallow
Their pleasure, and it will be in my power
To let them off the hook, and I might use
My power the generous way, maybe I won't,
It will be up to me, and if I abuse it, it will be
As I learned, before I understood I could learn
At all, when what informed my abbreviated
World was my mother and secret doubts about
My father, whom I've never missed, anymore
Than I'd miss what people do on Christmas Eve
If I'd never done it so memory reminds me
And shapes my sense of reading the future,
Forever the same as it is tonight, forever
The reckoning of what I've given myself,
Forever the knowledge I too can be cruel,
Because cruelty was done me and everybody
Knows it, and cruelty was done them but they
Don't want to talk about it, and maybe I
Believe in their kindness when they carefully
Ask if I have somewhere to go to celebrate
Christmas and I lie and answer yes.

The Fear Of Stopping

Nothing's better. When I call no one says
You've asked for me. I'm losing weight.
I didn't like the nights I'd stay awake and eat.
There wasn't much money, I was spending it
On gas to make the trips down 77, so I ate toast
With apple butter, slice after slice.
I'd take the Atarax the doctor prescribed
When I called and said I had to sleep
Or I was going to break down.
I needed strength to argue with family.
Therapy wasn't worth the expense,
My stepbrother Pat the urologist said.
He's a powerful man, not used to backtalk.
He takes his daughters to Aspen for skiing,
They're waitresses in their daily lives.
Pat's wife is a tobacco heiress, a pale blonde
With a sickly son from her first marriage.
She used to be a nurse in Pat's clinic.
That Thanksgiving I argued with him,
She kept peering out the window.
I don't know what bothered her, that I'd win
Or he would, neighbors would hear,
I don't know. She needn't have worried.
I didn't make a difference.

I dreamed about my stepbrother Greg:
Something happened to make him deaf,
And he didn't take it well, he turned helpless.
He's a salesman, a good talker.
Whatever it takes for him to get what he wants
Is what he wants. I dreamed his white shirt
With cuffs rolled up, hands holding his oblong head,
The only one like it in his family.
I've seen films of bands recording,
The technicians sit behind thick glass;
I dreamed myself behind glass.
I can't trust myself not to help someone
Who's worked against me if he's in trouble.
When I was sixteen he visited his father.
My bay mare Elfin grazed the pasture.
He asked if he could ride. I knew he'd use

The reins to balance, and they connect to the mouth.
He mounted bareback, she was fat and slick,
And he almost fell but saved himself
Grabbing the reins. I couldn't tell him
What to do. He was a young man lucky
To be born with satisfying knowledge.

Now everything's slowed down. I used to ride
Elfin to logging roads and gallop hard as I wanted.
I remember such flat smooth stones
On those trails, we'd pass over them fast,
And I'd glance down wondering what I'd do
If one stuck in her shoe. I remember the arch
Of her thick neck, I remember thinking about
Her mouth, softening my grip so my hands
Could follow her head's motion: I'd been drilled
In the importance of paying attention.
You had to if you wanted to run.
The horse was proof I could take a chance
And ride home clean. I knew the cardinal
Taking flight from a branch could startle Elfin
And make her swerve. I knew an old fencepost
Could mean a strand of wire to tangle
Her bony legs and cut them. I knew
It mattered where I balanced, so I worked to lean
At a forward angle. I remembered the charts
I'd studied in books that showed how the center
Of gravity shifts as you pick up speed.

No one calls to talk about you. If you think of me,
You don't tell the nurses. You can't remember
The name of the state where you visited me.
Or maybe they don't hear you right: maybe
You didn't say "Out there," maybe you said "Ohio."
You're tired of people who can't understand.
That's why I've stopped calling. I'm tired too.
In a quiet room where people are standing,
If someone's heart pounds, I can hear it.

Horses are like that. The scalloped muscle
Between the forelegs shivers a little, in rhythm.
Are they getting you up in the wheelchair?
We can't tell the nurses what happened.
We'd scare them off, and we need help.
We're animals too. We run till something snaps
And we fall, and as in the stories about racehorses,
We try to rise, we have to be stopped.
Not to save us, but so we can die without
Proving a point: we shouldn't've had to run
So hard. But we loved to believe in our rider's
Pleasure until it seemed it came from us,
The love of running, what our legs
Could manage, fear of what would happen
If we gave up—which, after all, would be nothing.

Redbud

Despite what she said,
I do not resemble an angel.

I am more like the redbud
Next to the driveway.
Three big limbs snapped
Under snow after budding
Early and hung by strips
Of bark and raw wood
Like white muscle
Until the night my friend
Who's leaving town forever
Tore them away in the beam
Of my car's headlights.

That's the kind of favor
He does me, no matter
How much it hurts
The tree to keep its shape.
So I don't thank him
For touch--only the idea.
He can't take that with him,
And I let it grow
Like the volunteer tomato
Vine I found in the compost
Back of the house in Roanoke—
Early 60's, it must've been,
A summer evening, news
Of war still a flash
At the corner of the eye
Just before blindness—
And I don't remember
Who told me it wouldn't
Bear fruit, some adult good
For destruction, the hammer
Of fact and experience,
But I returned to the dark
Mold of the compost pile
Where the strand of tomato

Vine curled slavishly
As a naked girl and slowly
Touched it to death
From the roots up.
It came loose in my hand
With a sigh,
And by the time I buried it
Again it was soft all over,
Limp with the loss of
Something—not soul,
But simpler than water.

I was a child who wanted
The earth to spring with life.
I wanted a dozen babies
When I grew up. I wanted
A stable of horses. I wanted
A garden of a thousand
Orchids. I wanted drink
For my talkative throat.
I wanted to put my hands
Everywhere. I wanted
A pebble in my pocket
And a friend to show it to,
And I kept getting worse.

To volunteer is to offer
Oneself for nothing—
Words for your own reason,
Always the same one:
I give you more than money,
A belief that unpaid debt
Can last forever as honor,
The circular logic of holding
Out. The tomato vine's
Scrawny flower proved
Everything, then less
Than nothing, shame
Of falling for the hoax:
It would be my first lesson

In love, repeated, reliable
As the turn of the seasons,
Cold to warmth, the brittle
Leaf to the seed, and my
Mother coached volunteers
In charity fundraising,
Said if they do the job
You're lucky, don't expect
Work when you don't pay
And don't think about why
They volunteer: of course
It's the wrong reason.
They want a bad idea,
And so did I, my borrowed
Notion of sex as trade:
It's yours, take it, you owe me
The price of desperation,
But boys and men turned
Away anyway, bland workers
In the foreign economy
Of late morning dream,
Guarding their shovels
Closely, staring into
Craters to the lava core.

I have lived in this house
Long as I can. The redbud
Tree may have sprung up
By the fence as a deer
Appears by the roadside
At night, poised for the leap
Into your radiator, its last
Moment of grace collapsed
In a clumsy tangle of blood
And fur. It might've been
Fair for my friend to clear
The damage the storm did.
I would've let it wither.
I keep the evidence around.

Since I have no religion,
It is not catholic
When I wish for penance
At the foot of the idol.
It is sexual,
But I was taught badly
And can only fail.
The statue's open palms
Do not squeeze shut
In reflex of ecstasy,
The eyes' marble shells
Exude no holy proof,
But the halo of blame
Clasps my skull
And the voice that will
Not speak utters
Its disappointment
So I can't talk back,
Only suffer
The heat in my skin
Like spirit, the male
Name for the full heart,
Cleansed of pleasure's
Indelible burden,
Footprints damp,
Leak down the thigh,
Resurrection.

She was wearing a coat
And a wool scarf
And she was late
To the reading
And she asked the right
Questions afterwards
So I wanted to know
Her name and it was
A name I'd heard
Twenty years ago
When we all feared
Dying young.

They dumped me,
She said. *I was sick*
For two years and they
All dumped me.
It was closing time
In the library and the young
Man who was frightened
Of me when we met and more
After I read the poem
With the word *fuck* in it
Seven times urged us out
The door into the parking lot
And we sat on the curb
Pretending to be
Graduate students again,
So hungry for poetry
We read it anywhere
Aloud, a cause, a politic,
To force poetry on the world
No matter how pissed off
It got, and it would,
Because the world hates
Truth, we believed,
And poetry says the truth,

And sometimes I still
Love to think it will happen,
The blossoming of the poem
Over graph paper peaks
Of the city skyline
Like the nuclear bomb
I used to have nightmares
About, though really it was
I feared everything
And there had to be a way
To end it, if not the fear
The world, which was
Smaller and cleaner,

With blue oceans,
Sweetmeat fishes,
Rocks you don't throw,
And magnetic crabs

As in the dream
Of the victory of poetry
The woman who went mad
Will read the woman
Who stayed sane a poem
From a wrinkled scrap
Of paper, handscrawled
In pencil, and the error
Of the poem will amount
To its genius, mention
Of angels real for once,
She is not faithful
But literal to the vision

Under the fluorescent tubes
Of the parking garage
Where no one would suspect
The end of the world
Beginning, visitation
Of the ghost of love,
Who made us sick
And went away
And married someone else
And is not forgotten
And only half-hated
And followed in dream
As children are told
Guardian angels haunt them
And does not grow younger
But is not on medication
And still has teeth
And can focus his eyes
And remember what to say
Next in conversation.

I watched my friend tear
Broken redbud branches
And it might've been my body
In his hands and him leaning
Against it with all his weight
To make sure and it is no good
Now to say I remember
How wrong it is to be so lucky,
It is too late for us all,
We have had our success,
We are hungry for more,
We will be careful not
To articulate what we mean
As we drag the limbs
To the curb, and if clearing
The dying wood from the tree
Seemed to my friend
All the love he could give,
It's because I own too much
Already, blooming like measles
And paying for it, fever
Melting the snow
Breaking the branches.
The last passion is counting,
Taking the measure,
To figure the cost of life
Precisely, the revenge
Of accuracy, by now
All we deserve.

I haven't told him yet
How a woman called me
An angel. He'll just laugh.
He won't much like it.
He's leaving town for good.
It's the way of the world,
Plainly smug I can't
Change it, and I try.

A middle-aged woman
Appeared to me once
In a library in Tulsa
And read a poem
About angels.
Redbud burdened
To breaking by snow,
The dark blood
In my body drags me
Down with my friend
And the woman
Who was driven mad
By loss. She and I
Will lie miles apart
In the night together
Hearing him track
Our shared blood,
Sticky, dragging him
Down like love,
Which in fear he fled,
Dodging the cruel darts,
As I have, though I was
Slow, like the woman
Who went mad from loss,
As someday I will,
Feeling the weight
Of wings on my back,
Reaching to stroke
The feathers as no one
Else would dare to do,
Except perhaps the woman
Who made them grow,
Since no one we loved
Would stay and it was
Clear we needed to fly.

II.

The Transformation

It had been afternoon as long as I could bear.
I folded the newspaper and laid it on the floor.
All the stories were on government appointments—
Bad news, not surprising. The accompanying photos'
Grainy smudge smeared suits and hands and faces.
You grow up with the fact of men, on TV, on the radio,
And they seem to belong there, like carvings
No one considers art. You can wrest them out
Of your life if you must, but if you had to take them back,
You'd get used to it fast. They're an old habit.
If that tree in the front yard were bigger, something
About the trunk might remind you. If you spent
Enough time in that chair on the porch you might know
How they feel. I do. Unspeakable ache
In back and loin, from hardly moving and wanting
To run, or fly. Or flee. Birds, for instance, are arrogant.
They know what they can do. I hadn't read
The gardening column in the paper I'd set aside.
But it wasn't going to stop me from looking out the window
To late January and the leaves I didn't rake
And hose I didn't coil on the hook
And fluffed-out wren shrilling bill-wide answering
My canary. He lives in a cage on my dresser.
Every night I cover it with a folded sheet,
And he tucks his head into his feathers to sleep.
That afternoon—today, I mean—he was singing.
I laid the newspaper down. I had to get up
And stretch my legs. I needed to get out of the house.
I'd been reading about the nation's officials,
Thinking I understood, yet it had nothing
To do with me. First I was a fatherless baby. Then
I was a little girl who didn't like to play with children.
Then I rode horses. Then overnight, everywhere, forever—
Men. My stepfather and three stepbrothers.
Boys I did drugs with, boys I slept with. Men, truck drivers,
Factory workers, teachers, writers, religious cultists.
A student. Then nothing, not a knock or a touch. I was safe.
But it took time not to speak modestly, in euphemisms,
Talk to titillate eunuchs in some country I never heard of,

Now racked by controversy. That was my life
All those man-years, man-hours, hard labor wishing
I could rest, stop somewhere, not see muscular backs
Twisting out of t-shirts in darkened rooms.
That stolid fish-jawed man driving through the intersection
After the light's turned red is somebody's craving
For some reason, or the thick-waisted boys
Hanging out around the up-hooded pickup on blocks—
They're somebody's life besides their own.
I needed to get out of the house. I'd been reading
The newspaper, classifieds, boring sports scores.
I stood on my feet. I passed across polished hardwood,
Someone heavy trying to be light.
The way I experience gratitude is to open my arms and walk
Through walls, and today when I tried it I stepped out of a mob,
A past of seashells, pasta shells, heel marks
On tile, and I don't know how all the men
Who'd harmed me happened to be gathered
In a room hung with plaid and brocade,
Solicitous and repelled as if it were our last week to live
And we were vomiting blood. But they were, formal
As ever, the reason I'd driven them to destruction.
I needed a laugh. So there I was, walking
Through walls, picking my way past a tapestry of skulls,
Moving faster as a stretch of dusty pavement
Opened up ahead, closing my ears to the circular song
Of my own breath and fast-drawn hope and nobody
Blocking me by accident and no terrified
Certainty I could only get so far, so slow.
There was no longing: only reproach.
I rose up off of the sofa that afternoon and walked
Through everything in my way. I wouldn't live in a house
I couldn't get out of, just that easy, and proud, too,
Like losing money night after night at the poker table
And finally winning a hand, or scoring a point
In an argument with a stranger.
I laid the newspaper on the floor and walked out
And dreamed and told everything I could
Before I had to start making it up, and that was the end
Of the sense I could make anyone understand.

The Auction

2 1971 Eisenhower Proof Dollars/Mint Case,
Bicentennial 1775/1875 Lex/Concord Medal,
Approximately 12 Plates, Okla. Shape Plate,
Baskets/Hen, Duck & Squirrel Shaped,
Shoe Stretcher, Horse Hames, Old Toy Trains,
Store Scales, Brass Hand Scale, Cotton Scale,
2 Accordian Folding Doors/New.
The stoplight shimmers crimson noon
And one last delivery van slips through
The intersection, loaded down low in back.
This turn tells it, north straight up Main
To the highway, past the plate glass shop
And the mobile home lot to the general store
Where the auction runs each Saturday,
Or east down Cedar, home: when she was a girl
And the car stopped for traffic, she'd tilt
Her face to the window's cool and dare her palm
To the door handle, fingers brushing chrome.
When the light flashed green, she'd lay her hand
In her lap. "I just want to bid on the bookcases,
'2 Large Wooden,' maybe they're the kind
You've wanted." The light changes, and he
Doesn't turn, doesn't speak, just drives,
Not fast as if she made him mad
But carefully, eyes ahead, hands steady
On wheel; she's sure he must be thinking
Over the mood he's been in lately, waking
Five mornings a week at five and working
Till dinner in his undershirt, smoking cigars,
Forgetting them glowing in the ashtrays—
And still getting nothing done, at least
To hear him tell it, and who else would know?
But sometimes she thinks he doesn't know
Why she goes to auctions and brings him too,
Doesn't see how sad he seems, how the sound
Of her voice reciting the auction notice—
3 Electric Organs, Plumbing Fittings/Cast Iron,
Meat Slicers, Fans, Adding Machines, Crib—

Brings him to listen as if she were far away
Or might head there if something went
Wrong: if, for instance, he said he'd go
To no more auctions. What then?
She wonders. It's almost worth his stooping
Walk a step behind when the bidding starts
And she nods on file cabinets and storm windows
And knows how he too wants file cabinets
And storm windows but wants no one
To know. Desire can't take him over, not
Like you'd expect from a young man with money
In the family. What could he think he has to lose?
He doesn't say. He does what he has to, like drive.

He steers into the parking lot south
Of the low building. The sun's an intolerable
Blister in the white sky. A row of pickups
Lines the orange pipe fence. It's hard to find
A parking space; there's one so near the road
They can't get out till nothing's coming.
She's watching, and he feels it on him
Like a hand and doesn't mind. A flat hand
On his arms and shoulders, his face, his own
Hands, bony back of his right hand—
"I don't want to go in there," he says.
"Wouldn't you rather go back home with me?"
It's either the auction with its fast voices
And straight faces or the silent house
In the shadow of Grand Avenue on Saturday
Afternoon and cool they've learned to doubt.
"I don't want to if you don't know why," she says
And keeps her hand behind her, quietly
Creeping to the angled latch—then,
When he says nothing, pops it and steps
Down into the heat to stroll in the masochistic
Dignity of tank top and tight jeans toward the arena,
To buy Oak Tables, Churn Paddle Top,
And New Faucet and even linger for the last item,
Portable Dishwasher, which goes for more
Than she thinks it's worth. She doesn't
Contend with other bidders but lowers
Her eyes and endures the auctioneer's.

Meridian

Tonight we saw a bobcat flash across a rutted red clay road
And disappear into bermuda grass gnarled in the undergrowth
Along the west edge of darkness. We heard coyotes' shrill yips
Crescent-sliced out of sight of Olaf's Anvil Ranch Farriery
Where we hauled Scottie and Jeanie to be trimmed and shod.

At dusk a flock of fat dark birds circled us, flight swaying
Through the treetops like grain sifting through mesh.
It was hard to tell what name to say until I spotted robin's rust.
Even that seemed too much to hope for, stolen wisdom,
Knowing what we traveled with, having glimpsed the fact.

Think of two middle-aged women with horses instead of children
And husbands and then think if we wanted it, or if, as Karen's friend
Gypsy says, we'd have men if we'd let them in—an idea Gypsy
Didn't hold when, last year, Dwayne left her and she wept so much
No one would talk to her. Tonight at Olaf's we backed the horses

Out of the trailer and walked them down the hill to his shop.
He'd been sick but he made small talk while he hammered the shoes,
Jeanie's first, and I noticed when he stroked her neck,
Not Scottie's: Jeanie's friendlier. Karen thinks Olaf caused her
Trouble with a man she loved, David: at forty, her only boyfriend.

But she kept the conversation going so you wouldn't think
She suspected him. Later she lay on the ground by her truck
To fix the wire on the running lights—on her side, arms
Over her head to reach the trailer hitch, and if she'd wanted,
If it hadn't been February in Meridian, Oklahoma, coyotes

Squealing scales inside out and Olaf red in the face bending over
Jeanie's turned-up hoof, she could've slept stretched like that.
She lay the way women lie with men to sleep, except for reaching away.
Which she didn't have much reason to know, I thought,
Before the last pale glaze faded from the horizon and Olaf

Finished the shoeing and we wrote him checks for fifty bucks
And he said next time he'd swing by Karen's place on the way
To David's, which we'd hoped he'd say but with Olaf

You never know if he'll do you a favor. I thought so even before
We started talking about men on the drive back, mostly Karen

Because Karen likes to talk, and she said she'd never stop feeling
Hurt David didn't tell her what she'd done to make him mad,
He just stopped speaking, and I said, "That's what they do.
That's what men do when you argue with them," and she said,
"I don't know what they do." Maybe it was then the bobcat

Ran across the road. Or maybe I just want to think of that silver
Body, big-pawed and shaggy, fast to be so clumsy, wild to be so small.
I want to think of robins lowering the sky to mulberry branches,
Of living like animals, an end to talk I can't stop listening to.
At Karen's we led the horses to their stalls, threw them flakes of hay,

Straightened their blankets, filled their water buckets.
They ate staring straight ahead, as horses do. And Karen,
Standing in the driveway, hooded sweatshirt tugged up,
Holding buckets of feed for the morning, talked a long time.
I'm going to keep the details secret. I'll just say we might still be there

Under the cold furtive stars telling everything if Canadian geese
Hadn't flown overhead, so close we thought we felt their wings.
They honked, and it would've been funny in broad daylight.
Instead it seemed wrong, like maybe they were lost.
Then Karen remembered the pond east of the rise.

You can see it, she said, from Mehan Road. I said I needed to get
Home, and she headed toward the barn with the buckets.
"If I were married I couldn't do what I did tonight," she said.
"I'll see you tomorrow," I said. By the time I made it to the paved
Road the heater was starting to work. I had to stop because a pickup

Was traveling west on Mehan from the big pond, and then I wanted
To wait a minute, thinking maybe I'd see a skunk or a raccoon.
If I were married I couldn't sit in my car with the engine running
At the end of a dirt road waiting for bobcats and smoking cigarettes.
It wasn't a big deal, thinking it over before pulling onto Mehan.

I passed only one wobbling car before 177 and the Stillwater traffic.

Why There Are So Few Horsemen & The Qualities Necessary To Become One

—after Guérinière, École de Cavalerie

I.

It's rained all morning, a cold rain,
Not freezing, finals week, a student rushes by
Muttering *Stupid teacher*. He's probably right,
I say when he's out the door. I never saw him
Before so he can't mean me, but I don't want him
To hear me agree. I'm cynical as an oyster
And closed tight. I don't want anyone
To know what I've been reading on the Internet.
I close my office door and study the names
Of a friend's friends and their poetry,
And slow fear bleeds out of the screen.
Like I told a student I feel responsible for,
We hate what's too much like us or too little.
Guérinière invented shoulder-in,
And in *École de Cavalerie*, a slender volume
Bound in high gloss mustard yellow,
Reprinted only in part to accommodate
The rider of our time, who has no need
To train the coach horse, war horse, hunt
Horse, Chapter XI opens with a plate captioned
In script *L'Epaule en Dedans*, an engraving
Of a noble blaze-faced bay performing
The new movement which has come to mean
As much to dressage as the work between the pillars
Ever did. Guérinière struggled to establish
His practice in the art of riding of the early
Eighteenth century but did not enjoy acceptance
Till late in life. His achievements might be
Understood as a rule of the period's obsession
With order, yet dressage continues to be
Refined today according to the abilities
Of the types of horses currently popular,
German breeds rather than the Spanish
Favored in Guérinière's day, Andalusians
And Lipizzaners, thick-necked, short-backed,

Graceful at the airs above the ground
As the Hanoverians and Holsteiners imported
At great expense in the 1990s perform extended
Gaits with style and impulsion the earlier
Breeds could not have attained. The engraving
Illustrates the arched neck and weight displaced
Onto the haunches of a horse in extreme collection,
Ears flicked back as I've seen my mare's
In that reflective, intense gesture horses make
To prove they're not dumb animals.
The eyes show white at the corners.
The rider sports a longer stirrup than most
Prefer today, and a portly companion
Stands on the track, facing the viewer,
Hand on hip and left leg skewed in a style
We would mock today for its fey formality.
This afternoon I wasted an hour joking
With a graduate student and a colleague
About the French. The student said, *The English
Are French* and the professor corrected him,
The French are Norman. The student said
*It's more fun to say they're English so someone
Will say*—he imitated my colleague's Ivy League
Inflections—*The French are Norman.* Later
I said I don't care about origins, it matters to me
What happens now, faithlessness short
Of atheism for caring too little to disbelieve.
He changed the subject when I said—I couldn't
Believe how mildly—his thought was luxury,
A white supremacist's, male supremacist's,
When he said he writes of horses to think
Of horses in general and has never cared
For an animal. He said, *The conqueror creates
Art and war.* He spoke of warriors parting
The clouds beating drums and imitated hands
Beating drums. I've read that dressage was
Invented when war horses learned the airs
Above the ground for battle, also that the airs
Above the ground are too difficult for practice
In the theater of war. I prefer the latter theory.

I said I don't care about origins and later
Tonight opened the book by the inventor
Of shoulder-in. It teaches a lesson
About how I spent the day mourning the loss
Of a friend to what I consider faulty art, the taste
Of demi-connoisseurs, and I had to admit
That my friend I loved is perhaps not
The connoisseur I once longed to call him
Insultingly, but half that, half the insult
Or twice. I don't know. The theory is poetry,
Or poetry is the theory, and the rhythm
Of the horse's footfalls, which takes a student
Rider months or years to understand by feel,
Does not resemble the rhythm of language,
Which some say is more complex but they
Have not ridden dressage and probably
Would not enjoy it. Shoulder-in is a subtle
Exercise comparable, perhaps, to free verse
Form, though some who support the so-called
Traditional forms, older than free verse,
Which by now possesses lengthy tradition,
Would dismiss my observation as biased.
Traditionally it was performed as shown
In the engraving captioned *L'Epaule en Dedans,*
In severe collection, but today, partly
To accommodate the demands of beginners
And the belief that all disciplines must be refined,
It is taught at the working walk. I find it safe
But difficult on Jeanie, who does not stride up
Under her belly but crabs along carefully,
Likely to avoid striking herself with the iron
Of right hoof crossing left ankle, as represented
In diagrams. I imitate the diction of the translation
I purchased for an inflated price, a work
Frequently cited in recent books on dressage,
So the publisher's assumption must be
That those with previous knowledge are willing
To pay, in my case true. Shoulder-in at trot

Offers the sensation of flowing smoothly
Forward, bent, hands held to the inside,
The horse's neck curved slightly but not forced,
Which would be a fault. Observers ask,
What's that movement called? and I'm annoyed
To interrupt rhythm with conversation.
Stupid teacher, the student said, bolting
Into the rain, into the Business building
Next door, perhaps to flunk another final.
He seemed a promising young man.
I am a reclusive middle-aged woman
Who has taken to sizing up the bodies
Of promising young men and describing
Them in late night phone conversations
With my reclusive middle-aged woman
Friends, and it seems it was only yesterday
We could get our hands on them
As now I can only close my hands on reins.
Guérinière details their use
In Chapter VII, The Bridle Hand
And Its Effects, which I have studied
But did not find as amusing as Chapter VIII,
The Aids and Punishments Required To Train
Horses, in which he remarks that sharp spurs
Should not be used on restive horses
Because such horses will piss with rage.

II.

One must suspect young girls and middle-aged
Women with a passionate interest in horses
Of finding in them symbolic sexual equivalence,
And when one lives in Oklahoma the parallels
Between cowboys' lives and slumped demeanor
In the saddle are so obvious one dares not
Comment. Oklahoma City reports
The nation's highest incidence of obesity,
And Tulsa rates as twenty-second fittest city.
How such statistics are derived is not

Related in the public media. When one is left
Alone one may develop habits such as spending
Considerable time and money viewing
Pornographic websites. This pastime
Is more usual among men but women may
Take it up. A friend says her uncle pours
His morning coffee at the computer and types in
His credit card number for hours of downloading
Tricky graphics of fucking and sucking.
We disapprove without saying why.
I am not personally involved
In the sexual practices abbreviated BDSM,
Which, when I bored away September
Posting on a feminist website, I had trouble
Typing correctly and feared being exposed
As out of touch. One might imagine a woman
Straddling a fat man, from Oklahoma City
Or points west, and she might, if she knew
The story, dub him Bodacious, after the notorious
Rodeo bull of whom one may purchase videos,
Who threw a number of cowboys to death
Of fractured skull or spine in a brand
Of pornography not considered such by born-
Again Oklahomans, and she might rake him
With sharp spurs till he pisses with rage.
One might imagine her genitals wet
On the thick pad of fat either side of his spine,
Safe in comparison to the cowboys'.
That's the part she's playing, and he is akin
To Bodacious, though swapping ends is not
His skill but crawling. Today on the Net I read
About poetry said to describe sex in forced forms,
And tonight I'm imagining, imitating,
Whatever I thought was meant, since
No example was given. I am longing
Not for the poetry of sex in forced forms
But the resonance of love Guérinière
Seems to have understood in his saddling

And straddling of the Spanish breeds.
He advises the horseman to like horses,
Though he notes that few people do not.
I equate his observation to what people say today
About sex, including BDSM, but to piss with rage
During sexual congress seems to me messy
And political in its implications. I am courting
Disapproval to write this. I am attempting
To titillate myself and failing because,
Embarrassingly, I fantasize of sex
With resonance of love, skeptical as I am
Of its longevity beyond the moment, experienced
As I am in disappointments and dissatisfactions,
Why I'm writing at three in the morning
After a day on which I gave a final exam
And might've been called *Stupid teacher*
By someone out of my earshot, but I don't care
About origins, and am faithless in the art of sex—
But I sometimes wonder if the men I've loved
Would enjoy pissing with rage when sharply
Spurred. Or throw themselves against the manege
Wall, or stop suddenly and lie down.
It may truly be said that the proper use
Of the aids and punishments is one
Of the finest attributes of a good horseman.

III.

"A knowledgeable master said, with reason,
That the pillars give spirit to horses
Because the fear of punishment keeps
Those who are bored and lazy in brilliant action,
And calms those naturally hot and angry,
Because the action of the piaffe, a regular,
Sustained, and elevated movement,
Makes them pay attention.

"In the beginning attention must be given
(When putting a horse in the pillars)

To attach the cavesson ropes so they are short
And of equal length so that the horse's
Shoulders are level with the pillars
And only the head and neck are above them.
One must then move behind the croup
With the long whip and remain far enough
Away there is no chance of getting kicked.
One then puts the horse to the right
And to the left by using the long whip
On the ground, sometimes on the rump.
This teaches him to cross the legs
And gives him the fear of punishment.
Attention must be given to making horses
With a sluggish croup and no movement
In the haunches kick in the pillars.
Everyone is not of this opinion, and most say
That one must never teach a horse to kick."

IV.

I wish I could show you the diagrams.
You could marvel, as I do, at the correct
Placement of the four irons, the oval moons
Of the hooves, in *renvers* and *travers*,
Translated in this edition to haunches-out
And haunches-in. You might fancy the *volte*,
Demi-volte, not to be performed by demi-
Connoisseurs. Guérinière often uses
A word that requires a special footnote, first
In the chapter on the temperaments
Of horses and the cause of their indocility.
It is descriptive of cowardly horses,
Caragnes, a variant of "carrion,"
Used as invective. The spur is *l'eperon*.
The long whip is *la chambrière*. Switch,
La gaule, a birch rod. *La longe* is a long
Cord. The spike, *le poinçon*, is a wooden

Handle with an iron point on the end.
The dock-piece, *la troussequeue*,
Is a leather instrument used around the tails
Of horses performing the high airs—
Pesades, mézair, courbette, croupade, balotade—
To make the horse appear to have a larger
Croup and prevent the tail from swishing
In the rider's eyes. I wish I could show you
The engravings. I wish I could ride
A Spanish horse leaping and kicking out
Behind. I would stay on, I would stick
In the saddle, my legs splaying to the ground,
In the air of love, the resonance, not forced
Forms, trained at the cost of years of my life,
The cost of years of my horse's life,
Which he would be glad to give,
Not because I hurt him but because he loved
The slide of my pelvis against his spine,
A language subtler than French or German,
Nothing you can study by imitation
Though of course we mostly do imitate
What we see when we are young,
Crouching behind couples in movie theaters,
Sneaking novels from desk drawers,
Untwisting keys in rusty locks,
Getting our hands moist or worse,
Wiping the sweat or whatever it is away,
Worrying about the odor no one could
Smell because no one is close and when
Someone is, it's only a moment I wish
I could ride to the finish and salute.
I am thinking of the fat man in the City,
They call it here, late at night, no one
Will guess, everyone will go to church
Tomorrow, the manege, the square,
The *demi-volte*, and look, I've slipped a bit
Into his mouth, my hands are light
On the separate reins, he's able to rest
His weight into it without hurting either one
Of us, and I'm riding him like he'd kill me

If he could, war horse, untrainable,
In an art that does not thrive
On imitation, but who would imitate this,
Where I'm riding my horse, no one thinks
To look, the thick neck of the Andalusian,
The mane falling beside the ears.
I am practicing fine art, the Cavalry.
I am dreaming the impossible vision,
But what else is there when one has lived
So long unhorsed, or, as they say
In Oklahoma, *Doesn't know one end
Of a horse from the other*, and I slip
The length of my body to the end
Of the horse that does know one
From the other, and he rests his mouth
Artfully, champing the bit so foam flecks
His lips in the attitude of dressage, which,
In case you didn't know, means training,
Specifically training of animals.

Knowledge

The roads were icy last night.
I had to take books to the library.
The asphalt glittered like a department
Store, and I've learned all I can about
What happened to you. I thought
I could restore you if I knew the secret
Words—like being a child and believing
The tale of the door that opens
On command. So much power is suddenly
In your hands, you rush to try it out.
You hurry upstairs to the bedrooms,
Where the doors close and keep you out.
Tonight the rooms are empty. You have to
Pull a door shut yourself to make the test,
Quietly: no one can know what
You're attempting. They wouldn't like it,
They're afraid you could go anywhere.
You speak the words softly. Too soft,
They don't work. There's the painted
Slab of wood, doorknob brittle with rust,
Skeleton key sagging in the hole,
Just as it was. You wish you could shout,
This door is hard of hearing, but times
Have changed, the old magic isn't
Good anymore except for stories.

You wouldn't've wanted me to drive
Last night. You used to turn on the weather
Report if I had to go across town. I'd say,
Why not look out the window?
Maybe there were distances inside
Your head even then you couldn't cross.
You needed the dry little man in the suit
Pointing to paper clouds with a stick.
You trusted the one who had made it
Into the living rooms of the city.
Some of those doors were closed to you,
No matter what you said. No wonder
You wouldn't listen to me. You know
What happens to the talkative one
Gesturing toward the pages of a book.

You know when she does her rain dance
The crops wither. You know when she falls
In love she ends up pregnant with no
Husband. You know when she tries to cure
The sick they get thinner, their eyes turn up
Accusingly, their breathing clogs,
And it turns out best they don't get well
Because they'd try to take revenge.

The Sign Of The Cross

Fat Back to Me ASAP Chris Headley of National Cremation
    Foundation scrawled on the fax
In black ink thick enough to bead rain like car wax. In the South of
    my childhood, fatback seasoned beans,
Collards, and my grandmother's stealthy lips in the kitchen after her
    stroke, when the family scandal—
She ate it raw—shamed me into wondering what was wrong. What
    would it do to you? Kill you?

How? Germs? Worms? If you've already had a stroke, who cares?
    Chris Headley did not mean
To invoke a homely cuisine but to urge me to return the form
    consigning
My mother's body to heat that reduces human flesh to fit
    in a plastic box—
The contract specifies that besides direct flame, "pulverization" is
    required—

Which, when I'm not so tired, I'll drive to Charlotte to pick up. The
    letter t lies same as the letter x.
One straight pencilstroke, another crossing. Handwritten t equals
    handwritten x tipped up, the sign
Of the cross, and you might think that because I grew up in the
    South I know
A lot about that kind of thing. Maybe you think I've worn a cross
    on a chain,

Silver engraved with a man's dead limbs; at least I might've given
    one, deep in cotton batting
To be lifted by some female relative—*my mother*—from a box
That wouldn't hold radius and ulna, let alone skull and femur. But
    if you knew me better,
You'd know that on this night when I want to think of something
    decent

To say about my family, now all gone but me, I mostly remember
    that none of us worshipped
Jesus, and my mother's favorite description of the falsely pious was
    He lives at the foot of the cross.
That is my great good fortune, of which I have seldom boasted.
Avenging memory of hardship, I've neglected to mention what it
    punished.

It seemed obvious to me—but not everyone is me, or my mother,
    who, fifty years ago,
Played a mean boogie piano and stomped her foot, size eleven five
    A, on the floor
By the soft pedal without once touching it. Irreverence in women is
    not suffered
By men like my stepfather, now also hospitalized, fluid on his heart,

Which is not to say he had any use for the cross either. You could've
    loved him for it
If not for what made him complain, when Sara pointed to his line
    on the death certificate
And warned him not to sign my line instead, "It ought to be enough
    for me to sign."
She said, "If you were paying it would be."

On the form I faxed back to Chris Headley, the space where I wrote
    "Daughter"
Over the direction "Relationship to Deceased" was large enough to
    inscribe
What she remembered of me this summer. "You don't like me,"
    she said—
The whim of stroke, to knock out everything for the sake of
    weakness,

Perhaps mine, or hers all along; and may I choose so my friends
    outlive me, unlike hers,
Who will not be attending the funeral that will not be held as she
    did not attend theirs
That were: not one of them set out to be callous or a traitor.
They made pacts, they parted, they meant to live up to the good of
    sworn design.

My mother is dead. I say it out loud, again. Clot of blackened ivy,
    stem, and bone,
Not like before, for real this time, and each new day I take my time
    recalling.
Mounded white ash like flour for bread, she could be anybody,

Victim of king or farmer, final measure of love's unmixture with
    money.

Free of the twisted body and brain shot full of glue, it can't hurt her
    to take the blame.
I, off the hook for once, am riding my mare in the October sun,
    innocence quivering
Through all our muscles, up hill and down, her knees through tall
    grass, moths rushing,
As if my mother could see us by shading her eyes with her hand.

When I stop beside her she has questions, a joke, only a little praise.
We are practicing sport we always loved, something hard we can try
    to understand.
We can have our differences of opinion and no one will be
    destroyed.
My mother is not anywhere—not the clouds or the earth,

Plastic box or crematorium, her sheer remains—she had wasted in
    anemia—
Repositioned in the chamber by whomever works there, perhaps
    someone with better penmanship
Than Chris Headley, who perhaps got stuck with the worst job
    because of it,
As things go in the opposite of heaven, not hell but the everyday,
    the day she was not there,

Really, to complain I'm not winning in the shows but I heard her,
    and I tried.
She is not on a cross or in a casket and she is not in the thoughts of
    those who never knew her.
Almost all who did are not anywhere either. Nonetheless we
    squabble over the finer points
Of my ankle position and whether it makes sense to sink money
    into boots and camcorders

When maybe the whole problem is needing a horse with more
    natural talent.
She approves when the weeds are mown, the poison of wild
    geranium and Virginia creeper,

And it's possible to see my mare's hoofprints in the dust and prove
    categorically
Who's right about whether her hind legs crossed in the *travers*, a
    movement

Like everything in heaven, requiring patience and a wait to perfect,
    and talk with no one listening.
How can such infidels be so true? Only when one of us has
    disappeared.
I would say it's all right but it's not all right. I say she's forgiven me
    but there's no proof.
I dismount to set up the little jumps called cavaletti, the long bar
    secure in the notch of the cross bars,

And there it is again, as in *Fat Back to Me*. The way I speak to the
    problem implicit in the x
Is to nudge my toe in the stirrup, and rise to the saddle and reins,
    and trot over the set of rails so long it's like floating,
The mare's joints flexing in a sign that can be turned any way you
    need to read it,
And death offered without promise, especially of forgiveness of the
    sin of omission

That slips its rhythm like a thrown shoe when someone is so far lost
The living wait long for her dying, grief's initiation foreclosed well
    past prayer.

The Heron

Now another consideration emerges.
Other people need to stop hearing me
Talk. They haven't hardened to
The language of medicine. They
Think words like "demented" mean
What they usually mean, what
A vicious thing to call your mother.
I chatter constantly, I bear into the eyes
Of listeners, and their attention sinks
Into the eyes' tunnel, deeper than I
Can count. That's not how my mother's
Gaze moves. Hers is surface, no longer
Shifted to one side, but casting for
The familiar. Someone gave me a book
On birds with a photo of a heron
Crouched on a rock. Specks floated
In the water around it. The caption
Claimed the bird planted them as bait.
When the fish rose to swallow them
The bird would take the fish, and,
Presumably, the specks too, or
Perhaps the bird moves faster than
The fish, and the bait is forgotten.
When people have strokes, they forget
What they're doing, what they reached
For, held in their hands and mouths.
It happens when they're zipping a child's
Jacket to play in the first snowfall,
Or after two weeks of arguments
With a spouse who ran out of money.
If they're fetching in the day's bills,
The letters scattered in the driveway
May remind you of the bait the fish
Didn't eat: the next fish strikes, next
Passerby picks up the letters, no one
Has bothered to enclose a check, but
The heron is busy with the brain
Of the first fish, dipping his long beak
In, so the second fish lives, though
The bait was disappointing: only life
Inside. That's what signed the letters.

If a woman has children, when her
Stroke takes one side, the state won't pay
For someone to tend it. That's what
The children do, in honor of their birth.
There were childhood days when tulips
Bloomed, the sidewalk rumbled
With tricycle tires, and the maples
Sent down whirling seeds, two wings
Spread like a heron's. Other people
Don't ask for the story. They think
They already know the details: mother's
Need dovetails with her children's adulthood.
Look at them upright, earning money,
They take satisfaction in dropping bait
On the water. They scoop up even
The smallest fish, several will hardly
Fill the stomach. For years they've been
Careful to order mother to preserve her
Well-being: *it's not good for you to lie*
In bed for months, it's not good for you
To be tied in a wheelchair, it's not
Good for you to pee through a catheter,
It lets the bacteria in. There's a shadow
At the door, it's nursing home staff.
She wants you to teach your mother
A riddle: *why do little girls grow up*
To be social workers? She says your
Mother will know the answer, it arises
Like bubbles from a punctured lung.

Fish have small brains, no one claims
They think much. Birds have small
Brains, some people claim they're
Very smart. They plant bait on water,
They wait on the rock, they watch with
Round yellow eyes, and they strike,
Long necks unfolding before you
Can blink, needle beaks plucking

The silvery minnow, a fish men use
To bait their hooks and wait and
Watch for something bigger. A bird
Wouldn't bother to argue for weeks
Over something its offspring had done.
I haven't read if birds have strokes.
One minute you might spot a heron
On a rock, sun glinting on the bait
Around it, the bird's neck furled
To strike. Then the wings open.
They frighten the fish honing in
On the speck in the water, the fish
Turns tail and makes way to safety,
And the heron falls, just like my mother.
Its eyes freeze open, just like my mother's.
But there's a difference. Its children
Don't know it. Even if they're nesting
In nearby trees they don't care what
Happened. All they see is another bird
Drowning. There's nothing they can do.

Vivisect

¢

Invert the starfish.
Its muscular points
Contract to resemble
A nerve-damaged hand.
Workers in mirror shops
May be thus injured.
But the scars show.
The underside
Of the starfish is
Clear of marks, unless
It comes from ocean
Shores littered
With broken glass.
You could open the disc
Of the ocre star or sea bat
With a crescent-moon
Sliver of green bottle,
Paring the five spiny
Arms, directing
The shard's edge
To the mouth where
The stomach protrudes.
With practice, you
Can pin down the slender
Snake star or intricate
Basket star, which walk
Without tubefeet,
A mystery to investigate:
Slice the muscled arms.

But you might hesitate
To crack the carapace
Of the mud turtle.
It exudes a musky
Smell, and bites.
You'd need sharper
Instruments, a helper

To assist in restraint,
Forced opening
Of the marginal scutes.
You'd need hammer
And chisel to undo
The hinged plastron
And check the gut
For carrion
On which the mud
Turtle feeds. The effort
Involved in this procedure
Might outweigh your
Satisfaction in knowing.
Or you might persist,
Your fingers entering
The turtle's entrails.
Open it, tug up the folds
Of leather where the head
Withdraws, or did.
The turtle isn't dead
But will be soon.
Meanwhile, you watch
A winding-down and do not
Describe it to your helper.
There are no words
For it you'd repeat.
What's undone is done.

⊗

Bob wanted to write *a fiction.*
He *had a novel in him.*
He'd heard at a conference
Realism was passé.
Scholars delivered
Papers on *popular culture.*
A man in khaki pants
And a shirt from Sears
Attributed *the death*
Of the short story

To sound bytes
And *Sesame Street*.
By dinner Bob had made a friend
Who ordered expensive wine.
Bob tried it
And found it good.
So were the blue corn
Tortilla chips. So was
The woman on his sleeve.
Her first conference, he told
His friend, and when
Either man mentioned
Her name, his voice
Grew husky as stalks
Of maize. She called them
Darling. She said she was
Sweet on them both.
Bob preferred to *keep*
His *several lives separate*—
He told the woman
He never quite took to bed.
Realism, however, was dead.
He would say, if pressed,
His memory is no good
With details. He refused
Realism less politely
Than the woman he'd seduced
With prophylactic care.

®

The recently fashionable
Art of feng shui suggests
The flow of blood in the body,
Analogous to ch'i, and any
Text on arranging wind
Chimes and mirrors
To direct what Westerners

Describe as "energy"
Might be remindful
Of vivisection in diagrams
Of houses cross-sectioned from
Above. If the East has lately
Imitated Western style,
As for instance in reports
Of Japanese women
Breaking ankles
In falls from platform shoes,
The West has consumed
Eastern philosophies,
Assimilating them into usage
Supporting Western customs.
English volumes on feng shui
Include passages on aura,
What every form radiates,
Felt by passing the hands
Near, allowing the palms
To rise or fall as sense
Dictates—too strong a word,
Better for getting at
The impulse to dissect.
"Body" feng shui suggests
Phrenology but is more
Detailed, interpreting
Shape and placement
Of facial features:
Eyebrows, for instance,
Assume characteristic angles
With lyrical names—
The *long-living star*,
Sign of talent and sexual
Appetite. The *sleeping tiger*,
Appearing angry
But underneath
Friendly and ambitious.
The *dragon, machete,*
Willow leaf, broom.
Feng shui addresses
What pop psych books

Call body language:
"Hands in the pockets:
People who do this
Want to hide weakness."
Someone of this habit
Might change his posture
To perform vivisection,
Or write a fiction, or imitate
The gestures of another
He wishes to impress,
The divine mirroring
We find flattering,
Consciously or not,
Which will likely turn out
Destructive to the stream
Of ch'i within,
Sinking to si ch'i,
Sadness or depression,
Diagnosed according
To Western custom
Not by divining or dowsing
But psychiatrist and DSM,
Treated with pharmaceuticals
Creating side effects:
Dizziness, bizarre
Dreams, absence of sexual
Desire, corrected
With other pharmaceuticals
Creating other side effects,
Some potentially lethal.
Once you've gone this far,
You may consider
The risk well worth it.
You could die anyway,
Closed or open, and the death
Of the psychiatrist's client
May seem to him or her
Not so alone

And less chaotic
Due to the acknowledged
Danger she or he
Attempts to sign away.

⇔

This is as good a time
As any to engage
The question of the terms
Of modernity and whether
Postmodernism avoids
And/or eliminates them.
We may take as the definition
Of the modern the assumption
Of metanarrative, the belief
That the world cannot be
Known related in comforting
Story form, endowing us
With identity, and if
Postmodernism depends
On the interlocking
Of local language games
So identity does not exist,
The male friend who says
Borderline Personality Disorder
Is so named because
Its sufferers do not
Recognize boundaries
Does not trace this habit
To its source as described
In the metanarrative of the DSM,
Fear of abandonment,
Which I've experienced
But the boundaries
I recognize seem real,
Belonging to others.
It may be that females
Are not perceived by men
I would diagnose with

Narcissistic Personality Disorder
As possessing boundaries.
In retrospect it interests me
That my pleasure increases
When friends arrive
Unannounced, as if
Transgression of boundaries
Were requisite to my pleased
Belief that I am desired.
Or, to put it another way,
Transgression of that sort
Becomes my version
Of respect. Do you believe
I'm analyzing interlocking
Language games
Informed by suppressed
Loyalty to metanarrative
As manifested in "life choices"
And "behaviors useful
For material gains"?
Through my use of punctuation
I'm implying knowledge.

∃

I doubt I could	*sleep with you.*
I think I would	*need Viagra.*
You are	*so very intimidating.*

I am *making all of this up.*
It is no longer *in my voice.*
It is no longer *confessional.*
It has become *imagined indictment.*
It has entered *the realm of speculation.*
It will become *a dream come true.*

∴

My biological father, son

Of a right-wing radio commentator
Of the 1950's, believed
In the metanarrative of God
And family, and though I was his
Firstborn, my name does not appear
In the volumes of *Who's Who*
In which he's listed until the 70's,
When he died or stopped submitting
Information with a fee.
My mother recognized his nickname
In an article about a mansion,
But when I do a net search,
Possibilities spill down the screen.
To hire a private detective,
A "dick," seems excessive.
Acquaintances urge me to seek truth
Or a lawsuit, but there are limits
To my wish to participate
In the terms of modernity,
Though Judith Butler, responding
To accusations that her application
Of Foucauldian analysis undermines
Feminist activism, has said
That the most radical act
Of postmodernism is to extend
Those terms to the previously excluded.
A friend likes to tell of a foal born
Through the fence. The mare
Had backed against it to give birth,
Maybe for shade, and all long hot
Oklahoma summer day the foal
Had tried to nurse, and failed.
So by the time my friend found them,
The panicked mare and the foal
Stretched out barely breathing,
The dehydration was too advanced
To reverse. I told my friend I was
Born through a fence. She said,
I'm sorry, but I have to change
The subject. I can't write that

Without feeling I'm being mocked.
And desiring to insinuate
Some other level of parody
Into what is otherwise pure self-pity.

√

To "confess," to "indict,"
To "vivisect."
Could you do it to me?
Could you "insist"?
Me in the college town
Burger joint, arguing
You shouldn't leave,
We'd gone to a "late lunch,"
And you said *I'm going*
To do it. Scalpel,
Please. I'll hold still.
I want to be rid of
That fluttering muscle
In the hollow beneath
My right eye.
I will demonstrate
The downiest touch
On the several layers
Of dermis. It will be
Difficult because
I can't see what I'm cutting,
I operate by *feel.*
I am showing respect
For your boundaries
By dismantling the local
Language of which
You disapprove,
Including: *Feel, Adultery,*
Confessionalism, Bad Manners,
Sorry To Have Missed You,
Take Care. I believe

You intended to make me
Feel better. "You"'ve seen
Nothing yet but are about to,
As I slide the blade
Through the layers
Of dermis to access
The muscle I've considered
Injecting with pharmaceutical
Botulism—trade name *Botox*—
Though I would lose
The ability to *squint*.
Sometimes I wake
And stare in the mirror,
Not your face
I watched so deliberately
I could draw it into
A scary cartoon,
And the skin beneath
The right eye is bluer
Than the skin of hedgehogs,
Puffy, as if the twitching
Twittered on all night,
Collecting a small pool
Of lactic acid—*no doubt*—
Which I will release
As I etch my skin
With the scalpel
For "you." I do it for "you,"
Carve away evidence
Of injury, for "you,"
Who said *I'm going to do it*
And did. If "your" hands,
"Your" fictional "hands,"
Possessed the gift
Of divining, you could pass
The palms over my face
In this form, cut-away,
Like upholstery
In a showroom
To expose the springs

That will support "your"
Spine, and they would
Rise, as with sha ch'i,
Or si ch'i, as they once
Would've risen with sheng
Ch'i, all of which
I laugh at because
You'd expect me to
And what else is there
With the horizon between "us"
And your acquisition
Of knowledge, true
To the fashion of "our" time,
Which is all you have
To count on, what you know
After all you've said,
And your travels,
And the dreams
The impractical believe.

+

I tell friends
What I read
About vivisection
In concentration camps
But they already know.
They change the subject
To baseball and grow
Animated describing
Pitcher and batter,
How one leads the other
Until the ninth inning
And everyone
Goes home exhausted.
Back to biology class,
Boring, except for
Pregnant rabbits,
The name given to

Women at Ravensbrück.
A cottontail
Bounds down the road
In front of my speeding
Car and I hit the brakes.
If I was pregnant,
I'd never tell.
I wouldn't let anyone
Know it made me
Sick. I wouldn't let
Anyone know what I
Wanted to eat.
I wouldn't have a husband
Run to the store
And buy what I wanted
With his friends forced
To settle for cutting
Dead things, searing
Their nostrils
With formaldehyde.
You're not going to
Believe this, but the day
I went belly up
I said I wanted to be
Pregnant, and it was
Such a good idea
I was nobody's
Business from that day
Forward. The gates
Opened, and, as with war
Crime trials, the criminals
Insisted accusation
Harmed them. They'd lived
Cheerful lives
Untainted by regret.
Nobody would speak
If I walked away,
As down the courthouse stairs,
Exonerated in word,
Examined inside,

Exiled from love,
Whatever it was,
And I knew
I hadn't seen
From outside
Where instruments
Glistened near the tear
Ducts of lovers
I never called
By that name,
Even in jest.

Acknowledgments

Grateful acknowledgment to the editors of the journals and anthologies in which these poems first appeared, often in slightly different form:

American Poetry Review: "Redbud"

Crazyhorse: "Morning Snowfall," "The Fear Of Stopping," "Christmas Eve, 1997"

Dominion Review: "Knowledge"

Gulf Coast: "Only A Little"

Indiana Review: "For My Mother's Sleep," "The Heron"

Louisville Review: "The Sign of the Cross"

Michigan Quarterly Review: "The End of Anything"

My Business Is Circumference: Poets on Influence and Mastery (Paul Dry Books): "Media"

Salt Fork Review: "Competition," "The History Of Sexuality"

Spoon River Poetry Review: "The Auction"

Stand Up Poetry: An Expanded Anthology (University of Iowa Press): "Tracy and Joe."

Third Coast: "Neurological Progressive Care"

TriQuarterly: "The Transformation"

photo by Dinah Cox

Lisa Lewis's previous collections are *The Unbeliever* (Brittingham Prize), *Silent Treatment* (National Poetry Series), *Story Box* (Poetry West Chapbook Contest), and *Burned House with Swimming Pool* (*American Poetry Journal* Award). Her work has appeared in many literary journals and anthologies, including the *American Poetry Review, Kenyon Review, American Literary Review, Fence, Rattle, Missouri Review, Washington Square,* the Pushcart Prize anthology, and two editions of *Best American Poetry.* She directs the creative writing program at Oklahoma State University and serves as poetry editor for the *Cimarron Review.*

New Issues Poetry

Gerry LaFemina, *The Window Facing Winter*
Steve Langan, *Freezing*
Lance Larsen, *Erasable Walls*
David Dodd Lee, *Abrupt Rural; Downsides of Fish Culture*
Lisa Lewis, *Vivisect*
M.L. Liebler, *The Moon a Box*
Alexander Long, *Vigil*
Deanne Lundin, *The Ginseng Hunter's Notebook*
Barbara Maloutas, *In a Combination of Practices*
Joy Manesiotis, *They Sing to Her Bones*
Sarah Mangold, *Household Mechanics*
Gail Martin, *The Hourglass Heart*
Melinda Markham, *Having Cut the Sparrow's Heart*
Justin Marks, *A Million in Prizes*
David Marlatt, *A Hog Slaughtering Woman*
Louise Mathias, *Lark Apprentice*
Khaled Mattawa, *Tocqueville*
Gretchen Mattox, *Buddha Box; Goodnight Architecture*
Carrie McGath, *Small Murders*
Paula McLain, *Less of Her; Stumble, Gorgeous*
Lydia Melvin, *South of Here*
Sarah Messer, *Bandit Letters*
Wayne Miller, *Only the Senses Sleep*
Malena Mörling, *Ocean Avenue*
Julie Moulds, *The Woman with a Cubed Head*
Carsten René Nielsen, *The World Cut Out with Crooked Scissors*
Marsha de la O, *Black Hope*
C. Mikal Oness, *Water Becomes Bone*
Bradley Paul, *The Obvious*
Jennifer Perrine, *The Body Is No Machine*
Katie Peterson, *This One Tree*
Jon Pineda, *The Translator's Diary*
Donald Platt, *Dirt Angels*
Elizabeth Powell, *The Republic of Self*
Margaret Rabb, *Granite Dives*
Rebecca Reynolds, *Daughter of the Hangnail; The Bovine Two-Step*
Martha Rhodes, *Perfect Disappearance*
Beth Roberts, *Brief Moral History in Blue*
John Rybicki, *Traveling at High Speeds* (expanded second edition)
Mary Ann Samyn, *Inside the Yellow Dress; Purr; Beauty Breaks In*
Ever Saskya, *The Porch is a Journey Different from the House*
Mark Scott, *Tactile Values*
Hugh Seidman, *Somebody Stand Up and Sing*
Heather Sellers, *The Boys I Borrow*